Landscape Poets

THOMAS HARDY

Landscape Poets

THOMAS HARDY

Selected and introduced by Peter Porter
Photographs by John Hedgecoe

Weidenfeld and Nicolson   London

Contents

SCENES AND SITUATIONS

POEMS 1912–13

WAR POEMS, POEMS ON PUBLIC THEMES, COMEDIES, LAMENTS AND FAREWELLS

Introduction

Today Thomas Hardy's reputation as a poet is the equal of, and possibly greater than, his standing as a novelist. It was not always so; indeed, for many years before his death in 1928 and afterwards, he was considered the classic example of the novelist who took up poetry only to demonstrate that success in the one art disqualified a man from success in the other. By the time Hardy was recognised as a poet he was already an old man. His poetical flowering in extreme old age is a remarkable enough phenomenon, but it should not blind us to another fact about his career – he had been a poet all along.

Poetry was Hardy's first as well as his last love. He turned to the novel for purely financial reasons. He had no private means, and from the time that he abandoned architecture for writing, he was obliged to earn his living by composing novels. It is true that poets as dissimilar as Tennyson and Swinburne made a lot of money from their verse, but Hardy was not of their social class and quite unknown when he set out. Fiction was forced upon him, and he served it long and with dogged devotion. This is not to assert that his achievement as a novelist is less considerable than as a poet, or to question work undertaken with reluctance (left to his own wishes, Shakespeare might have written sugared romances in rhyming stanzas after Ariosto, such as *Venus and Adonis*, instead of his commercially inspired plays). In any scale of values, *Tess of the D'Urbervilles*, *Under the Greenwood Tree* and *Jude the Obscure* would rank as master-pieces. My point is that behind the long series of novels which ended with *Jude* – indeed, woven into the scenes they contain and the world they project – is a tapestry of poetical feeling and symbolism which the foreground of events never completely obscures.

Hardy was a poet *sui generis* and remained so through a very extended literary life. There are even ways in which his originality as a poet tie in with his temperament as a novelist. It is not simply the case that after the scandal of *Jude*, he abandoned novel-writing with relief and returned to a purer art form, which had always been waiting in the wings. Hardy wrote poetry at most points in his life, though he kept it by him instead of publishing it in the heyday of his career as novelist. His *Collected Poems* include many pieces with dates up to thirty years before their publication. Writing venues appended to poems issued in the new century, such as Westbourne Park Villas, speak of his early residence in London in the 1860s, and many a verse has a footnote, 'reworked from an old draft'. Always the novelist's eye was enriching the poet's vision. Hardy, as he says in his poetic masterpiece, 'Afterwards', was a great noticer of things. What made him a supremely original poet, even a revolutionary one, was the very quality which worried

T. S. Eliot, his truth to facts. His poetry is a hymn to subject-matter, a vindication of the real, the observable and the precise object-in-place, not just, as with most poets, a set of characteristic scenes and situations. Hardy achieved such realism in the face of considerable difficulty: the times he lived in, their prevailing theories of what was proper to literature, and his own pronounced archaism of diction and form. Surely no great poet employs so much fustian – special poetic words, inversions of speech order and jingling rhymes – and yet sets before his reader such a recognisable world, true to the last naturalistic detail.

Hardy's poetry shares with his novels a landscape (and what is often forgotten) a townscape. The landscape has become world famous due largely to Hardy's renaming of locations of the West Country for his series of Wessex novels. Wessex has never been a properly delineated area of Britain since Anglo-Saxon days, and Hardy's cunning adoption of this far-off and numinous name is part of his supreme skill as a myth maker. His sense of an upper structure of Fates and Gods, in immortal session above ordinary life in rural Dorset, Devon and Somerset, might have foundered if Hardy had stuck to the real names of the places he set his stories in. While every reader knows that Casterbridge is Dorchester, Christminster Oxford, Budmouth Weymouth, and Exonbury Exeter, and can guess that Abbot's Cerne must be Cerne Abbas, Lulwind Cove Lulworth Cove etc., the persistent renaming acts as a steady mythologising force, a magical form of distancing and romanticising realistically recorded places, people and happenings. The effect is not dissimilar to the frisson which Tolkien admirers obtain from consulting a map of Middle Earth crowded with resonant and numinous names. When you reflect that Tolkien's is a made-up cosmos and Hardy's only an overpowering instinct for evasion, you appreciate that Hardy's unconscious was advising him well. He was tooling-up to be a major artist. His verse is less consistent in adopting inventions and parallels for familiar West Country names than his prose. He is often content to let the real name stand in a poem. Pilsdon is mentioned often in the poems, for instance, and you can climb to the top of Pilsdon Pen and survey Western Dorset from its highest point of vantage, as I have done. Generally, Hardy lets a real name stand when the place has only a local fame. Bigger and better-known locations are usually given a different cognomen. Since the new names are usually transparent adaptions, Hardy's purpose may sometimes seem obscure. Apart from a sense of anxiety in his own person, justified in a writer from the lower middle class who had not been educated at a university, the purpose of this renaming must be the one given above – to help purge his work of everyday, journalistic reportage and invest it with timeless significance.

The placing of his poems in real, identifiable locations does not mean that one can find an area, photograph it and thereby understand better the poem set in it. It is the flow of sympathy and its opposite, the menace of nature, which is still mysteriously there in the Hardy country and which the camera can catch. Also the relationship between imaginative art and the reality from which it springs is never a simple one; nor has it outstanding lineaments just waiting to be shown. With a camera parts of Hardy's mix can be isolated subtly – less a matter of specific locations than of characteristics of cloud shapes, hillsides, tracks and roads, and the unchanging cattle and sheep in the fields. Much that Hardy was familiar with in Wessex has altered, particularly in the seaside towns he wrote about almost as often as he did the villages, farms and country churches. But the permanent features can be got into the lens: thrushes and sparrows washing and prinking, hawks and blackbirds on the wing, thorns, bracken and wild flowers, dew on a graveyard and snow waiting to fall.

> Drops on gate-bars hang in a row
> And rooks in families homeward go. . . .

is one sort of Hardy vision. 'O the opal and the sapphire of the wandering Western Sea' is another. But the chief job of the photographer charting the world of Hardy's imagination is one of empathy. He must enter into a state of immanence, find images which are more than a backdrop to human events. He must picture the soul of a place and render its indifference to human endeavour as much as its support of emotion. What Hardy wrote about Egdon Heath, 'a place perfectly concordant with man's nature – neither ghastly, hateful, nor ugly; neither commonplace, unmeaning, nor tame, but like man, slighted and enduring; and withal singularly colossal and mysterious in its swarthy monotony' must be reproduced in black-and-white plates. And the people who are always a focus for Hardy in his poems cannot be present in the photographer's images. Or, at least, they can only be supporting characters, not *dramatis personae*, since a book of pictures is not a film and Hardy's poems are not plays.

John Hedgecoe has found a Wessex which is not an ordnance survey of Hardy's poetry. Pilgrims of the novels and, to a lesser extent, the poems, will not be able to use his pictures to track down the very scenes of Hardy's works of art. But this is no loss, since what an artist makes of reality is never the same as reality recorded in no more than its own everyday clothes. The critic with a complete guide to Hardy's Wessex before him will still lose what makes the art he admires worth esteeming, if he thinks that visible reality is the same as invented reality. There are nearly 900 pages of poetry in Hardy's *Collected Verse*, and well over half of this total was born imaginatively out of the sights and scenes of Wessex as Hardy knew them for the second fifty years of the nineteenth century. Yet, not even in Max Gate and its garden, home of Hardy and his first wife for so long, nor in Cornwall, in the village of St Juliot and its church or by the cliffs of Boscastle and in Pentargan Bay, or along the valley of the river Valency, will he find a twenty:twenty equivalence of place and poem. The camera, like the poet's genius, must conjure the spirit which resides in scenes and human feelings. That is what *genius loci* means, and that is what the photographs in this book have tried to reincarnate.

Hardy the realist can be served by photography, but literary criticism must concern itself with different aspects of the real. I began this introduction by insisting on Hardy's revolutionary stance as a poet, and finding it located in his attitude to subject-matter. It is interesting to compare Yeats and Hardy, near-contemporaries though Yeats was the slightly younger man. Yeats may be greater than Hardy, though I would not be sure of that myself, but he is very much more 'poetic' than Hardy is. This is not just a matter of technique. Hardy, who can be clumsy in his verse, was the more conscious technician in his writing, and is always more aware of the forms and contrivances into which he moulds his thought. Like many self-taught artists, he adored the classics and the mainstream of tradition, and wrote poems consciously as exercises in received forms. It was what his instinct as an artist told him to put in those forms by way of subject and feeling which was revolutionary, and which caused the forms themselves to alter as he used them. Technical prowess is invisible in Yeats. We know that Yeats writes well because there are no seams in his poems; he has total eloquence. But there is no visible rhetoric or any use of difficult forms which call attention to their own virtuosity. Hardy's verse-making is self-consciously inventive; he wants the reader to see how his poems are made. It is this, quite as much as his fondness for archaic language and inversions of colloquial word order, which earn him his reputation for old-fashionedness. Hardy stands out as an example of the master-craftsman, a writer whose poetical joinery is as well done as the best work of a cabinet-maker.

Hardy was just as interested in writing inspired poems as Yeats and Eliot were. For him, inspiration could not be sought at the expense of truth to reality, or through avoidance of unpleasant and hard-to-deal-with human facts. He is very high on the list of poets whose determination is to make eloquent the hard options and surfaces of everyday life. That is why he stands apart from modernism. Modernism is a sort of aestheticism; it appreciates that much of human existence cannot be made lyrical and therefore avoids it. It also tends to leave out the connectives and bridge passages of consecutive thought, confining itself to high and musical moments. Hardy is not like this at all. He puts everything in and he somehow manages to be lyrical at the same time. His use of lines of varying length is remarkable in this context. He can sustain extremely long lines without losing rhythmical tension or drifting into prose, as the poems of the 'In Tenebris' sequence show.

Hardy's poetry has its limitations. It tends to return to moods of regret and melancholy. The recurrence of graveyards, ghosts and fantasies on departed spirits is almost too much of a good thing, though this mode also serves him for some of his masterpieces. The many poems which burst from him in 1913, after the death of Emma, his first wife, show how the imagination can go over and over the same ground – the Cornish scenes of their courtship for example – and discover new and even more moving instances of an obsessional haunting. Hardy's atheism is sometimes perplexing, since it includes a great deal of God-bothering, and inclines towards pagan concepts such as an enskied court of immortals and the hand of fate. He sees little hope of redemption, through charity or God. He can be almost self-parodying in his stoic hopelessness, but people of our epoch, whose despair is internalised, do not do well to be critical of Victorian writers who had human misery on a vast scale before their eyes.

All in all, it is amazing how much ordinary life Hardy gets into his poems. A designer could fit out a dozen films of life at almost all levels of society in late Victorian England from a close reading of Hardy's verse: the churches and their music, their architectural follies and Gothic restorations, the gardens, the conservatories and the public walks, the seaside esplanades, the coaching inns and village pubs, the gates, stiles and tracks of farm land, the market towns with traders, auctioneers, and professional people, and, lastly and most importantly, the gentry and their dependants, being born, courting, marrying and not marrying, and so coming at last to death. Each poem adds a glint to the mosaic which his corpus of work presents to the careful reader. And, like a mosaic, none of it has lost its brightness. Pain and happiness alike linger on in places where once they were felt. Hardy picks up a skeleton of a lady's sunshade on Swanage cliffs. It immediately suggests to him a scene from the past:

> Where is the woman who carried that sunshade
>   Up and down this seaside place? –
>   Little thumb standing against its stem,
>   Thoughts perhaps bent on a love-strategem.
>   Softening yet more the already soft face!
>
> Is the fair woman who carried that sunshade
>   A skeleton just as her property is,
>   Laid in the chink where none may scan?
>   And does she regret – if regret dust can –
>   The vain things thought when she flourished this?

Hardy is especially the poet of indoor scenes. Perhaps one should say indoor scenes with a strong sense of the presence of out-of-doors. Dozens of poems record desolate moments in studies, sitting-rooms and libraries, perhaps with rain streaming down the windows, or with curtains drawn on a strange sorrow or a moment of recognition of isolation. Compare 'The Self-Unseeing' and 'During Wind and Rain'. Both are interior pieces, typical of the home entertainment of Victorian households, when people played and sang round the piano, and when there was always someone who could execute a dance measure on the fiddle. There is a lamp-lit sadness about such parlour scenes which appealed to Hardy. Depression and loss are his great subjects and he loves to show them against settings of conventional conviviality. In Hardy's day, people still played viols and violins in parish churches in Dorset, in a tradition unbroken since Jacobean times. 'The Self-Unseeing' is Hardy's picture of a time of happiness separated from him by death and probably estrangement:

> Childlike, I danced in a dream;
> Blessings emblazoned that day;
> Everything glowed with a gleam;
> Yet we were looking away!

A whole novel is locked in the economy of that last sentence. 'During Wind and Rain', although a longer and more elaborate poem, is more straightforward in tone. Here are the summer vistas of pleasure – singing, tending the garden, picnicking and finally prospering and moving to a grander house – yet time has them all in thrall and will take them away, just as it granted them in the first place. Hardy is master of the telling phrase and sentence: 'sick leaves', 'white storm birds', 'the rotten rose ripped from the wall'; and of the cold vision as people are reduced to names inscribed on gravestones or memorials: 'Down their carved names the rain-drop ploughs'. Over and above the ordinary features lovingly preserved in this poem is a wider and deeper power, as if of melancholy turned to godhead, which accords well with the resonant title, which Turner might have chosen for one of his ambiguous impressionist paintings.

Hardy's poetry did not develop very much and he writes in *Winter Words*, his last and posthumously published collection, of the same town and country matters which had occupied him as a young man. There was a public (abstract even) side to his poetry which linked it to his fondness for philosophy, for the ancient world and stoic attitudes. I have not included any pages from his huge drama *The Dynasts*, which Hardy regarded as his masterpiece, and which dealt at great length with his rather tiresome obsession with Napoleon and his times. Hardy was a dramatist in his novels and in his poems, but he was no playwright. *The Dynasts* can impress one cumulatively, but it is not interesting in excerpts. However, his power of employing abstractions in poetry, always a difficult thing to do, is deeply impressive. It shows in a famous early poem, 'Neutral Tones'. Two lovers feel the early blight which destroys love and even hope. Hardy does not tell us why such despair attends love, but he suggests that it is a process of the due working-out of fate. Nature roundabout expresses its complicity in the scene – what Ruskin called 'the pathetic fallacy'. The whole poem acts as a summing-up of Hardy's view of human happiness:

> The smile on your mouth was the deadest thing
> Alive enough to have strength to die;
> And a grin of bitterness swept thereby
> Like an ominous bird a-wing....
>
> Since then, keen lessons that love deceives,
> And wrings with wrong, have shaped to me
> Your face, and the God-curst sun, and a tree,
> And a pond edged with grayish leaves.

Even more impressive is 'Before Life and After', which Benjamin Britten made the culmination of his beautiful Hardy cycle of songs, *Winter Words*. The whole poem is conducted in abstractions, yet it is as urgent and deeply etched as any poem dealing in concrete images. The theme could be said to be Hardy's *idée fixe* – 'the disease of feeling' bringing pain to a world cursed by fate. This is a very hard theme to handle but Hardy is both proverbial and immediate in his verse. The tragedy located in Darwinian progress has never been so beautifully or economically charted: the two stanzas quoted contrast 'primal rightness' with man's state today.

> If something ceased, no tongue bewailed,
> If something winced and waned, no heart was wrung;
> If brightness dimmed, and dark prevailed,
> No sense was stung.
>
> But the disease of feeling germed,
> And primal rightness took the tinct of wrong;
> Ere nescience shall be reaffirmed
> How long, how long?

Mingling melancholy notions, abstract concepts and the visible world about him was Hardy's speciality, as in one of his best-loved poems, 'The Darkling Thrush'. It begins as a grim winter spectacle, but surprisingly modulates toward hope. The agent of that hope is the singing of the bird, a gift of nature which pre-dates 'the disease of feeling'. It is significant that he is no young springtime thrush, but 'aged ..., frail, gaunt and small ... in blast-beruffled plume'. Like the poet, he has scant cause for joy, but he may know instinctively of some spring of hope the rational poet is unaware of.

> So little cause for carolings
>   Of such ecstatic sound
> Was written on terrestrial things
>   Afar or nigh around,
> That I could think there trembled through
>   His happy good-night air
> Some blessed Hope, whereof he knew
>   And I was unaware.

Mankind's pride in its power of reasoning takes a harder knocking from Hardy than from any English poet since the Earl of Rochester.

The masterpieces among Hardy's poems of departure are 'The Last Signal' and 'Afterwards', his tributes to the passing of the Dorset dialect poet, William Barnes, and his imaginative vision of his own obsequies. The last signal of the title is a flash of sun on the old poet's coffin as it is carried to the graveyard, which Hardy likens to the wave of a familiar hand. In 'Afterwards', Hardy asks us to remember him when he is dead in the same way that he remembered Barnes: by thinking of the natural sights he loved, the garden creatures he knew so well, and the sounds of parish and village which measured out his life. The new shoots of May, the dewfall hawk, the hedgehog, the full-starred heavens and the passing bell are all Hardy needs to build up an unforgettable picture of human sympathy. Hardy does not come to comfort easily, but when he does, he fills it with the amplitude of a major poet.

> If, when hearing that I have been stilled at last, they stand at the door,
>   Watching the full-starred heavens that winter sees,
> Will this thought rise on those who will meet my face no more,
>   'He was one who had an eye for such mysteries'?
>
> And will any say when my bell of quittance is heard in the gloom,
>   And a crossing breeze cuts a pause in its outrollings,
> Till they rise again, as they were a new bell's boom,
>   'He hears it not now, but used to notice such things'?

The greatest single spasm in Hardy's poetical life came immediately after the death of his first wife, Emma, in 1913. As Robert Gittings has pointed out in his biography of Hardy, the ways of a poet's creative imagination are not simple or direct. Theirs had not been a happy marriage and, indeed, the silences and alienation of the establishment at Max Gate must have been the model for many of Hardy's desolate indoor scenes. Yet Emma's death was celebrated in dozens of tender and regretful poems recalling the landscape and activity of their courting. Hardy had gone to St Juliot church in 1870 to supervise its restoration, and met there and courted Emma Lavinia Gifford, the rector's sister-in-law. More than forty years later, after Emma's death, those Cornish sights and scenes came back to Hardy and he poured out a stream of poems including 'After a Journey', 'At Castle Boterel' and 'Under the Waterfall'. Few poets have been gifted with utterance whereby the lost past is regained, the sad refusal of life to live up to its hopes is redeemed through a weird form of haunting:

> Woman much missed, how you call to me, call to me . . .

> I see what you are doing: you are leading me on
>   To the spots we knew when we haunted here together . . .

> Up the cliff, down, till I'm lonely, lost,
>   And the unseen waters' ejaculations awe me.
> Where you will next be there's no knowing,
>   Facing round about me everywhere,
>   With your nut-coloured hair,
> And gray eyes, and rose-flush coming and going.

These poems, which Hardy published as *Poems of 1912–1913*, bear the latin epigraph *Veteris vestigia flammae*. In his essay *Hardy's Virgilian Purples*, Donald Davie argues for Hardy's being considered a great poet of loss, a true inheritor of the classical tradition. He also points out that Hardy's resourcefulness as a poet was firmly based on true models, and that his experimenting in stanza shapes and complex rhythms makes him far from the naïve village recorder that superficial reading of his weaker works suggests.

Because there is little development in Hardy's verse over the long span of its creation – good and bad pieces come from all decades and themes reappear at every stage – a selection may be arranged in any number of ways without doing violence to the thread of his thought or producing any harsh dissonance by placing mature work beside juvenile. A thematic arrangement presents certain difficulties, but is the best way to anthologise him in the long run.

Accordingly, I have put those poems which I believe are Hardy's best into four categories. The first I have called *In Wessex: Rural Pictures*, which I think is self-explanatory. The second is entitled *Scenes and Situations*. Most of these are set in Wessex, though some are not attached to any territory. They are mostly poems about people and situations, and range from London to the seaside resorts of Dorset, Devon and Cornwall. They are as much indoor as outdoor pieces. The third category, *Poems 1912–13* is more self-contained, referring to Hardy's grief at the death of his first wife. The fourth category brings together Hardy's many general poems, including his comic extravaganzas, and his incomparable laments. It is entitled *War Poems, Poems on Public Themes, Comedies, Laments and Farewells*.

It is nearly 150 years since Hardy's birth and his vindication is complete. I could wish that it were more soundly based, however. He is the subject of dozens of cranks and obsessionals, and for every good biographical or exegetical work about him, such as Gittings's *Young Thomas Hardy* and *The Older Hardy* or Tom Paulin's study of the poems (*Thomas Hardy: The Poetry of Perception*), there are a dozen with assertive axes to grind. His force has been felt by each new generation of English poets since his death – firstly by Auden, then by Phillip Larkin and recently by Peter Redgrove's generation, and by Tom Paulin's. But I do not hear people quoting Hardy in the course of their everyday life, as thousands do his contemporaries, Rudyard Kipling and A. E. Housman. The great Hardy revival is still slow in getting underway, and the public may well feel that approval by academics is a further reason for them to keep off. If so, they would be wrong. Hardy belongs to the whole English-speaking world, and not just to those who know the West Country. Like most great writers, his is an indigenous talent, but it travels well. His vision went far beyond the cliffs of his native county. The places in which his art is rooted are wonderfully graphic in themselves, as photographs show, but his spirit must pass into the pictures from the poems. Once you have heard Hardy's unique voice, you will always welcome it back – even though his view of life is bleak and sometimes comfortless. There is a music in Hardy's poetry which calls out to be heard. One who heard the call was Benjamin Britten, and I would recommend any Hardy lover to hear Britten's cycle of nine songs, *Winter Words*. These two English geniuses here distil the most potent essences of their country. Hardy has such an effect on his hearers and readers. He brings a whole world before their eyes and makes them feel that they know it instinctively.

The Poems

IN WESSEX: RURAL PICTURES

Wessex Heights

There are some heights in Wessex, shaped as if by a kindly hand
For thinking, dreaming, dying on, and at crises when I stand,
Say, on Ingpen Beacon eastward, or on Wylls-Neck westwardly,
I seem where I was before my birth, and after death may be.

In the lowlands I have no comrade, not even the lone man's friend –
Her who suffereth long and is kind; accepts what he is too weak to mend:
Down there they are dubious and askance; there nobody thinks as I,
But mind-chains do not clank where one's next neighbour is the sky.

In the towns I am tracked by phantoms having weird detective ways –
Shadows of beings who fellowed with myself of earlier days:
They hang about at places, and they say harsh heavy things –
Men with a wintry sneer, and women with tart disparagings.

Down there I seem to be false to myself, my simple self that was,
And is not now, and I see him watching, wondering what crass cause
Can have merged him into such a strange continuator as this,
Who yet has something in common with himself, my chrysalis.

I cannot go to the great Plain; there's a figure against the moon,
Nobody sees it but I, and it makes my breast beat out of tune;
I cannot go to the tall-spired town, being barred by the forms now passed
For everybody but me, in whose long vision they stand there fast.

There's a ghost at Yell'ham Bottom chiding loud at the fall of the night,
There's a ghost in Froom-side Vale, thin-lipped and vague, in a shroud of white,
There is one in the railway train whenever I do not want it near,
I see its profile against the pane, saying what I would not hear.

As for one rare fair woman, I am now but a thought of hers,
I enter her mind and another thought succeeds me that she prefers;
Yet my love for her in its fulness she herself even did not know;
Well, time cures hearts of tenderness, and now I can let her go.

So I am found on Ingpen Beacon, or on Wylls-Neck to the west,
Or else on homely Bulbarrow, or little Pilsdon Crest,
Where men have never cared to haunt, nor women have walked with me,
And ghosts then keep their distance; and I know some liberty.

Lying Awake

You, Morningtide Star, now are steady-eyed, over the east,
    I know it as if I saw you;
You, Beeches, engrave on the sky your thin twigs, even the least;
    Had I paper and pencil I'd draw you.

You, Meadow, are white with your counterpane cover of dew,
    I see it as if I were there;
You, Churchyard, are lightening faint from the shade of the yew.
    The names creeping out everywhere.

The Farm-Woman's Winter

I

If seasons all were summers,
    And leaves would never fall,
And hopping casement-comers
    Were foodless not at all,
And fragile folk might be here
    That white winds bid depart;
Then one I used to see here
    Would warm my wasted heart!

II

One frail, who, bravely tilling
    Long hours in gripping gusts,
Was mastered by their chilling,
    And now his ploughshare rusts.
So savage winter catches
    The breath of limber things,
And what I love he snatches,
    And what I love not, brings.

The Third Kissing-Gate

She foots it forward down the town,
    Then leaves the lamps behind,
And trots along the eastern road
    Where elms stand double-lined.

She clacks the first dim kissing-gate
   Beneath the storm-strained trees,
And passes to the second mead
   That fringes Mellstock Leaze.

She swings the second kissing-gate
   Next the gray garden-wall,
And sees the third mead stretching down
   Towards the waterfall.

And now the third-placed kissing-gate
   Her silent shadow nears,
And touches with; when suddenly
   Her person disappears.

What chanced by that third kissing-gate
   When the hushed mead grew dun?
Lo – two dark figures clasped and closed
   As if they were but one.

We Field-Women

    How it rained
When we worked at Flintcomb-Ash,
And could not stand upon the hill
Trimming swedes for the slicing-mill.
The wet washed through us – plash, plash, plash:
    How it rained!

    How it snowed
When we crossed from Flintcomb-Ash
To the Great Barn for drawing reed,
Since we could nowise chop a swede. –
Flakes in each doorway and casement-sash:
    How it snowed!

    How it shone
When we went from Flintcomb-Ash
To start at dairywork once more
In the laughing meads, with cows three-score,
And pails, and songs, and love – too rash:
    How it shone!

Shortening Days at the Homestead

The first fire since the summer is lit, and is smoking into the room:
    The sun-rays thread it through, like woof-lines in a loom.
    Sparrows spurt from the hedge, whom misgivings appal
That winter did not leave last year for ever, after all.
      Like shock-headed urchins, spiny-haired,
      Stand pollard willows, their twigs just bared.

Who is this coming with pondering pace,
Black and ruddy, with white embossed,
His eyes being black, and ruddy his face
And the marge of his hair like morning frost?
      It's the cider-maker,
      And appletree-shaker,
And behind him on wheels, in readiness,
His mill, and tubs, and vat, and press.

Winter Night in Woodland

(OLD TIME)

The bark of a fox rings, sonorous and long: –
Three barks, and then silentness; 'wong, wong, wong!'
In quality horn-like, yet melancholy,
As from teachings of years; for an old one is he.
The hand of all men is against him, he knows; and yet, why?
That he knows not, – will never know, down to his death-halloo cry.

With clap-nets and lanterns off start the bird-baiters,
In trim to make raids on the roosts in the copse,
Where they beat the boughs artfully, while their awaiters
Grow heavy at home over divers warm drops.
The poachers, with swingels, and matches of brimstone, outcreep
To steal upon pheasants and drowse them a-perch and asleep.

Out there, on the verge, where a path wavers through,
Dark figures, filed singly, thrid quickly the view,
Yet heavily laden: land-carriers are they
In the hire of the smugglers from some nearest bay.
Each bears his two "tubs," slung across, one in front, one behind,
To a further snug hiding, which none but themselves are to find.

And then, when the night has turned twelve the air brings
From dim distance, a rhythm of voices and strings:
'Tis the quire, just afoot on their long yearly rounds,
To rouse by worn carols each house in their bounds;
Robert Penny, the Dewys, Mail, Voss, and the rest; till anon
Tired and thirsty, but cheerful, they home to their beds in the dawn.

"Where Three Roads Joined"

Where three roads joined it was green and fair,
And over a gate was the sun-glazed sea,
And life laughed sweet when I halted there;
Yet there I never again would be.

I am sure those branchways are brooding now,
With a wistful blankness upon their face,
While the few mute passengers notice how
Spectre-beridden is the place;

Which nightly sighs like a laden soul,
And grieves that a pair, in bliss for a spell
Not far from thence, should have let it roll
Away from them down a plumbless well

While the phasm of him who fared starts up,
And of her who was waiting him sobs from near
As they haunt there and drink the wormwood cup
They filled for themselves when their sky was clear.

Yes, I see those roads – now rutted and bare,
While over the gate is no sun-glazed sea;
And though life laughed when I halted there,
It is where I never again would be.

At Middle-Field Gate in February

The bars are thick with drops that show
    As they gather themselves from the fog
Like silver buttons ranged in a row,
And as evenly spaced as if measured, although
    They fall at the feeblest jog.

They load the leafless hedge hard by,
    And the blades of last year's grass.
While the fallow ploughland turned up nigh
In raw rolls, clammy and clogging lie –
    Too clogging for feet to pass.

How dry it was on a far-back day
    When straws hung the hedge and around,
When amid the sheaves in amorous play
In curtained bonnets and light array
    Bloomed a bevy now underground!

Voices from Things Growing in a Churchyard

These flowers are I, poor Fanny Hurd,
          Sir or Madam,
A little girl here sepultured.
Once I flit-fluttered like a bird
Above the grass, as now I wave
In daisy shapes above my grave,
          All day cheerily,
          All night eerily!

– I am one Bachelor Bowring, "Gent,"
          Sir or Madam;
In shingled oak my bones were pent;
Hence more than a hundred years I spent
In my feat of change from a coffin-thrall
To a dancer in green as leaves on a wall,
          All day cheerily,
          All night eerily!

– I, these berries of juice and gloss,
          Sir or Madam,
Am clean forgotten as Thomas Voss;
Thin-urned, I have burrowed away from the moss
That covers my sod, and have entered this yew,
And turned to clusters ruddy of view,
          All day cheerily,
          All night eerily!

– The Lady Gertrude, proud, high-bred,
          Sir or Madam,
Am I – this laurel that shades your head;
Into its veins I have stilly sped,
And made them of me; and my leaves now shine,
As did my satins superfine,
          All day cheerily,
          All night eerily!

– I, who as innocent withwind climb,
          Sir or Madam,
Am one Eve Greensleeves, in olden time
Kissed by men from many a clime,
Beneath sun, stars, in blaze, in breeze,
As now by glowworms and by bees,
          All day cheerily,
          All night eerily!

- I'm old Squire Audeley Grey, who grew
                Sir or Madam,
Aweary of life, and in scorn withdrew;
Till anon I clambered up anew
As ivy-green, when my ache was stayed,
And in that attire I have longtime gayed
                All day cheerily,
                All night eerily!

- And so these maskers breathe to each
                Sir or Madam
Who lingers there, and their lively speech
Affords an interpreter much to teach,
As their murmurous accents seem to come
Thence hitheraround in a radiant hum,
                All day cheerily,
                All night eerily!

Friends Beyond

William Dewy, Tranter Reuben, Farmer Ledlow late at plough,
        Robert's kin, and John's, and Ned's,
And the Squire, and Lady Susan, lie in Mellstock churchyard now!

"Gone," I call them, gone for good, that group of local hearts and heads;
        Yet at mothy curfew-tide,
And at midnight when the noon-heat breathes it back from walls and leads,

They've a way of whispering to me – fellow-wight who yet abide –
        In the muted, measured note
Of a ripple under archways, or a lone cave's stillicide:

"We have triumphed: this achievement turns the bane to antidote,
        Unsuccesses to success,
Many thought-worn eves and morrows to a morrow free of thought.

"No more need we corn and clothing, feel of old terrestial stress;
        Chill detraction stirs no sigh;
Fear of death has even bygone us: death gave all that we possess."

W.D. "Ye mid burn the old bass-viol that I set such value by."
Squire – "You may hold the manse in fee,
        You may wed my spouse, may let my children's memory of me die."

Lady S. – "You may have my rich brocades, my laces; take each household key;
    Ransack coffer, desk, bureau;
   Quiz the few poor treasures hid there, con the letters kept by me."

Far. – "Ye mid zell my favourite heifer, ye mid let the charlock grow,
    Foul the grinterns, give up thrift."
Far. Wife. – "If ye break my best blue china, children, I shan't care or ho."

All – "We've no wish to hear the tidings, how the people's fortunes shift;
    What your daily doings are;
   Who are wedded, born, divided; if your lives beat slow or swift.

"Curious not the least are we if our intents you make or mar,
    If you quire to our old tune,
If the City stage still passes, if the weirs still roar afar."

– Thus, with very gods' composure, freed those crosses late and soon
    Which, in life, the Trine allow
(Why, none witteth), and ignoring all that haps beneath the moon,

William Dewy, Tranter Reuben, Farmer Ledlow late at plough,
    Robert's kin, and John's, and Ned's,
And the Squire, and Lady Susan, murmur mildly to me now.

The Paphian Ball

ANOTHER CHRISTMAS EXPERIENCE
OF THE MELLSTOCK QUIRE

We went our Christmas rounds once more,
With quire and viols as theretofore.

Our path was near by Rushy-Pond,
Where Egdon-Heath outstretched beyond.

There stood a figure against the moon,
Tall, spare, and humming a weirdsome tune.

"You tire of Christian carols," he said:
"Come and lute at a ball instead.

"'Tis to your gain, for it ensures
That many guineas will be yours.

"A slight condition hangs on't, true,
But you will scarce say nay thereto:

"That you go blindfold; that anon
The place may not be gossiped on."

They stood and argued with each other:
"Why sing from one house to another

"These ancient hymns in the freezing night,
And all for nought? 'Tis foolish, quite!"

"– 'Tis serving God, and shunning evil:
Might not elsedoing serve the devil?"

"But grand pay!" ... They were lured by his call,
Agreeing to go blindfold all.

They walked, he guiding, some new track,
Doubting to find the pathway back.

In a strange hall they found them when
They were unblinded all again.

Gilded alcoves, great chandeliers,
Voluptuous paintings ranged in tiers,

In brief, a mansion large and rare,
With rows of dancers waiting there.

They tuned and played; the couples danced;
Half-naked women tripped, advanced,

With handsome partners footing fast,
Who swore strange oaths, and whirled them past.

And thus and thus the slow hours wore them:
While shone their guineas heaped before them.

Drowsy at length, in lieu of the dance
"*While Shepherds watched* ...." they bowed by chance;

And in a moment, at a blink,
There flashed a change; ere they could think

The ball-room vanished and all its crew:
Only the well-known heath they view –

The spot of their crossing overnight,
When wheedled by the stranger's sleight.

There, east, the Christmas dawn hung red,
And dark Rainbarrow with its dead

Bulged like a supine negress' breast
Against Clyffe-Clump's faint far-off crest.

Yea; the rare mansion, gorgeous, bright,
The ladies, gallants, gone were quite.

The heaped-up guineas, too, were gone
With the gold table they were on.

"Why did not grasp we what was owed!"
Cried some, as homeward, shamed, they strode.

Now comes the marvel and the warning:
When they had dragged to church next morning,

With downcast heads and scarce a word,
They were astound at what they heard.

Praises from all came forth in showers
For how they'd cheered the midnight hours.

"We've heard you many times," friends said,
"But like *that* never have you played!

"*Rejoice, ye tenants of the earth,*
And celebrate your Saviour's birth.

"Never so thrilled the darkness through,
Or more inspired us so to do!" ...

– The man who used to tell this tale
Was the tenor-viol, Michael Mail;

Yes; Mail the tenor, now but earth!–
I give it for what it may be worth.

A Bird-Scene at a Rural Dwelling

When the inmate stirs, the birds retire discreetly
From the window-ledge, whereon they whistled sweetly
And on the step of the door,
In the misty morning hoar;
But now the dweller is up they flee
To the crooked neighbouring codlin-tree;
And when he comes fully forth they seek the garden,
And call from the lofty costard, as pleading pardon
For shouting so near before
In their joy at being alive: –
Meanwhile the hammering clock within goes five.

I know a domicile of brown and green,
Where for a hundred summers there have been
Just such enactments, just such daybreaks seen.

Proud Songsters

The thrushes sing as the sun is going,
And the finches whistle in ones and pairs,
And as it gets dark loud nightingales
In bushes
Pipe, as they can when April wears,
As if all Time were theirs.

These are brand-new birds of twelve-months' growing,
Which a year ago, or less than twain,
No finches were, nor nightingales,
Nor thrushes,
But only particles of grain,
And earth, and air, and rain.

"I Am the One"

I am the one whom ringdoves see
    Through chinks in boughs
    When they do not rouse
    In sudden dread,
But stay on cooing, as if they said:
    "Oh; it's only he."

I am the passer when up-eared hares,
    Stirred as they eat
    The new-sprung wheat,
    Their munch resume
As if they thought: "He is one for whom
    Nobody cares."

Wet-eyed mourners glance at me
    As in train they pass
    Along the grass
    To a hollowed spot,
And think: "No matter; he quizzes not
    Our misery."

I hear above: "We stars must lend
    No fierce regard
    To his gaze, so hard
    Bent on us thus, –
Must scathe him not. He is one with us
    Beginning and end."

The Later Autumn

Gone are the lovers, under the bush
    Stretched at their ease;
    Gone the bees,
Tangling themselves in your hair as they rush
    On the line of your track,
    Leg-laden, back
    With a dip to their hive
    In a prepossessed dive.

Toadsmeat is mangy, frosted, and sere;
    Apples in grass
    Crunch as we pass,
And rot ere the men who make cyder appear.
    Couch-fires abound
    On fallows around,
    And shades far extend
    Like lives soon to end.

Spinning leaves join the remains shrunk and brown
    Of last year's display
    That lie wasting away,
On whose corpses they earlier as scorners gazed down
    From their aery green height:
    Now in the same plight
    They huddle; while yon
    A robin looks on.

At Day-Close in November

The ten hours' light is abating,
    And a late bird wings across,
Where the pines, like waltzers waiting,
    Give their black heads a toss.

Beech leaves, that yellow the noon-time,
    Float past like specks in the eye;
I set every tree in my June time,
    And now they obscure the sky.

And the children who ramble through here
    Conceive that there never has been
A time when no tall trees grew here,
    That none will in time be seen.

Wagtail and Baby

A baby watched a ford, whereto
    A wagtail came for drinking;
A blaring bull went wading through,
    The wagtail showed no shrinking.

A stallion splashed his way across,
    The birdie nearly sinking;
He gave his plumes a twitch and toss,
    And held his own unblinking.

Next saw the baby round the spot
    A mongrel slowly slinking;
The wagtail gazed, but faltered not
    In dip and sip and prinking.

A perfect gentleman then neared;
    The wagtail, in a winking,
With terror rose and disappeared;
    The baby fell a-thinking.

Birds at Winter Nightfall

Around the house the flakes fly faster,
And all the berries now are gone
From holly and cotonea-aster
Around the house.   The flakes fly! – faster
Shutting indoors that crumb-outcaster
We used to see upon the lawn
Around the house.   The flakes fly faster,
And the berries now are gone!

The Puzzled Game-Birds

They are not those who used to feed us
When we were young – they cannot be –
These shapes that now bereave and bleed us?
They are not those who used to feed us,
For did we then cry, they would heed us.
– If hearts can house such treachery
They are not those who used to feed us
When we were young – they cannot be!

The Rambler

I do not see the hills around,
Nor mark the tints the copses wear;
I do not note the grassy ground
And constellated daisies there.

I hear not the contralto note
Of cuckoos hid on either hand,
The whirr that shakes the nighthawk's throat
When eve's brown awning hoods the land.

Some say each songster, tree, and mead –
All eloquent of love divine –
Receives their constant careful heed:
Such keen appraisement is not mine.

The tones around me that I hear,
The aspects, meanings, shapes I see,
Are those far back ones missed when hear,
And now perceived too late by me!

SCENES AND SITUATIONS

Neutral Tones

We stood by a pond that winter day,
And the sun was white, as though chidden of God,
And a few leaves lay on the starving sod;
     – They had fallen from an ash, and were gray.

Your eyes on me were as eyes that rove
Over tedious riddles of years ago;
And some words played between us to and fro
     On which lost the more by our love.

The smile on your mouth was the deadest thing
Alive enough to have strength to die;
And a grin of bitterness swept thereby
     Like an ominous bird a-wing....

Since then, keen lessons that love deceives,
And wrings with wrong, have shaped to me
Your face, and the God-curst sun, and a tree,
     And a pond edged with grayish leaves.

A Church Romance

(MELSTOCK: *circa* 1835)

She turned in the high pew, until her sight
Swept the west gallery, and caught its row
Of music-men with viol, book, and bow
Against the sinking sad tower-window light.

She turned again; and in her pride's despite
One strenuous viol's inspirer seemed to throw
A message from his string to her below,
Which said: "I claim thee as my own forthright!"

Thus their hearts' bond began, in due time signed.
And long years thence, when Age had scared Romance,
At some old attitude of his or glance
That gallery-scene would break upon her mind,
With him as minstrel, ardent, young, and trim,
Bowing "New Sabbath" or "Mount Ephram."

She Hears the Storm

There was a time in former years –
    While my roof-tree was his –
When I should have been distressed by fears
    At such a night as this!

I should have murmured anxiously,
    "The pricking rain strikes cold;
His road is bare of hedge or tree,
    And he is getting old."

But now the fitful chimney-roar,
    The drone of Thorncombe trees,
The Froom in flood upon the moor,
    The mud of Mellstock Leaze,

The candle slanting sooty wick'd,
    The thuds upon the thatch,
The eaves-drops on the window flicked,
    The clacking garden-hatch,

And what they mean to wayfarers,
    I scarcely heed or mind;
He has won that storm-tight roof of hers
    Which Earth grants all her kind.

"We Sat at the Window"

We sat at the window looking out,
And the rain came down like silken strings
That Swithin's day.   Each gutter and spout
Babbled unchecked in the busy way
        Of witless things:
Nothing to read, nothing to see
Seemed in that room for her and me
        On Swithin's day.

We were irked by the scene, by our own selves; yes,
For I did not know, nor did she infer
How much there was to read and guess
By her in me, and to see and crown
        By me in her.
Wasted were two souls in their prime,
And great was the waste, that July time
        When the rain came down.

Drawing Details in an Old Church

I hear the bell-rope sawing,
And the oil-less axle grind,
As I sit alone here drawing
What some Gothic brain designed;
And I catch the toll that follows
        From the lagging bell,
Ere it spreads to hills and hollows
        Where people dwell.

I ask not whom it tolls for,
Incurious who he be;
So, some morrow, when those knolls for
One unguessed, sound out for me,
A stranger, loitering under
        In nave or choir,
May think, too, "Whose, I wonder?"
        But not inquire.

The Musical Box

Lifelong to be
Seemed the fair colour of the time;
That there was standing shadowed near
A spirit who sang to the gentle chime
Of the self-struck notes, I did not hear,
    I did not see.

Thus did it sing
To the mindless lyre that played indoors
As she came to listen for me without.
"O value what the nonce outpours –
This best of life – that shines about
    Your welcoming!"

I had slowed along
After the torrid hours were done,
Though still the posts and walls and road
Flung back their sense of the hot-faced sun,
And had walked by Stourside Mill, where broad
    Stream-lilies throng.

And I descried
The dusky house that stood apart,
And her, white-muslined, waiting there
In the porch with high-expectant heart,
While still the thin mechanic air
    Went on inside.

At whiles would flit
Swart bats, whose wings, be-webbed and tanned,
Whirred like the wheels of ancient clocks:
She laughed a hailing as she scanned
Me in the gloom, the tuneful box
    Intoning it.

Lifelong to be
I thought it.   That there watched hard by
A spirit who sang to the indoor tune,
"O make the most of what is nigh!"
I did not hear in my dull soul-swoon –
    I did not see.

The Whitewashed Wall

Why does she turn in that shy soft way
    Whenever she stirs the fire,
And kiss to the chimney-corner wall,
    As if entranced to admire
Its whitewashed bareness more than the sight
    Of a rose in richest green?
I have known her long, but this raptured rite
    I never before have seen.

– Well, once when her son cast his shadow there,
    A friend took a pencil and drew him
Upon that flame-lit wall.   And the lines
    Had a lifelike semblance to him.
And there long stayed his familiar look;
    But one day, ere she knew,
The whitener came to cleanse the nook,
    And covered the face from view.

"Yes," he said: "My brush goes on with a rush,
    And the draught is buried under;
When you have to whiten old cots and brighten,
    What else can you do, I wonder?"
But she knows he's there.   And when she yearns
    For him, deep in the labouring night,
She sees him as close at hand, and turns
    To him under his sheet of white.

The Five Students

The sparrow dips in his wheel-rut bath,
    The sun grows passionate-eyed,
And boils the dew to smoke by the paddock-path;
    As strenuously we stride, –
Five of us; dark He, fair He, dark She, fair She, I,
    All beating by.

The air is shaken, the high-road hot,
    Shadowless swoons the day,
The greens are sobered and cattle at rest; but not
    We on our urgent way, –
Four of us; fair She, dark She, fair He, I, are there,
    But one – elsewhere.

Autumn moulds the hard fruit mellow,
And forward still we press
Through moors, briar-meshed plantations, clay-pits yellow,
As in the spring hours – yes,
Three of us; fair He, fair She, I, as heretofore,
But – fallen one more.

The leaf drops: earthworms draw it in
At night-time noiselessly,
The fingers of birch and beech are skeleton-thin
And yet on the beat are we, –
Two of us; fair She, I.   But no more left to go
The track we know.

Icicles tag the church-aisle leads,
The flag-rope gibbers hoarse,
The home-bound foot-folk wrap their snow-flaked heads,
Yet I still stalk the course –
One of us. ... Dark and fair He, dark and fair She, gone:
The rest – anon.

The Wind's Prophecy

I travel on by barren farms,
And gulls glint out like silver flecks
Against a cloud that speaks of wrecks,
And bellies down with black alarms.
I say: "Thus from my lady's arms
I go; those arms I love the best!"
The wind replies from dip and rise,
"Nay; toward her arms thou journeyest."

A distant verge morosely gray
Appears, while clots of flying foam
Break from its muddy monochrome,
And a light blinks up far away.
I sigh: "My eyes now as all day
Behold her ebon loops of hair!"
Like bursting bonds the wind responds,
"Nay, wait for tresses flashing fair!"

From tides the lofty coastlands screen
Come smitings like the slam of doors,
Or hammerings on hollow floors,
As the swell cleaves through caves unseen.
Say I: "Though broad this wild terrene.
Her city home is matched of none!"
From the hoarse skies the wind replies:
"Thou shouldst have said her sea-bord one."

The all-prevailing clouds exclude
The one quick timorous transient star;
The waves outside where breakers are
Huzza like a mad multitude.
"Where the sun ups it, mist-imbued,"
I cry, "there reigns the star for me!"
The wind outshrieks from points and peaks:
"Here, westward, where it downs, mean ye!"

Yonder the headland, vulturine,
Snores like old Skrymer in his sleep,
And every chasm and every steep,
Blackens as wakes each pharos-shine
"I roam, but one is safely mine,"
I say.   "God grant she stay my own!"
Low laughs the wind as if it grinned:
"Thy Love is one thou'st not yet known."

During Wind and Rain

They sing their dearest songs -
He, she, all of them - yea,
Treble and tenor and bass,
  And one to play;
With the candles mooning each face....
  Ah, no; the years O!
How the sick leaves reel down in throngs!

They clear the creeping moss -
Elders and juniors - aye,
Making the pathways neat
  And the garden gay;
And they build a shady seat....
  Ah, no; the years, the years;
See, the white storm-birds wing across!

They are blithely breakfasting all –
Men and maidens – yea,
Under the summer tree,
    With a glimpse of the bay,
While pet fowl come to the knee....
        Ah, no; the years O!
And the rotten rose is ript from the wall.

They change to a high new house,
He, she, all of them – aye,
Clocks and carpets and chairs
    On the lawn all day,
And brightest things that are theirs....
        Ah, no; the years, the years;
Down their carved names the rain-drop ploughs.

The Garden Seat

Its former green is blue and thin,
And its once firm legs sink in and in;
Soon it will break down unaware,
Soon it will break down unaware.

At night when reddest flowers are black
Those who once sat thereon come back;
Quote a row of them sitting there,
Quite a row of them sitting there.

With them the seat does not break down,
Nor winter freeze them, nor floods drown,
For they are as light as upper air,
They are as light as upper air!

Molly Gone

No more summer for Molly and me;
    There is snow on the tree,
And the blackbirds plump large as the rooks are, almost,
    And the water is hard
Where they used to dip bills at the dawn ere her figure was lost
    To these coasts, now my prison close-barred.

No more planting by Molly and me
    Where the beds used to be
Of sweet-william; no training the clambering rose
    By the framework of fir
Now bowering the pathway, whereon it swings gaily and blows
    As if calling commendment from her.

No more jauntings by Molly and me
    To the town by the sea,
Or along over Whitesheet to Wynyard's green Gap,
    Catching Montacute Crest
To the right against Sedgmoor, and Corton-Hill's far-distant cap,
    And Pilsdon and Lewsdon to west.

No more singing by Molly to me
    In the evenings when she
Was in mood and in voice, and the candles were lit,
    And past the porch-quoin
The rays would spring out on the laurels; and dumbledores hit
    On the pane, as if wishing to join.

Where, then, is Molly, who's no more with me?
    – As I stand on this lea,
Thinking thus, there's a many-flamed star in the air,
    That tosses a sign
That her glance is regarding its face from her home, so that there
    Her eyes may have meetings with mine.

The Strange House

(MAX GATE, AD 2000)

"I hear the piano playing –
    Just as a ghost might play."
"– O, but what are you saying?
    There's no piano to-day;
Their old one was sold and broken:
    Years past it went amiss."
"– I heard it, or shouldn't have spoken;
        A strange house, this!

"I catch some undertone here,
    From some one out of sight."
"– Impossible; we are alone here,
    And shall be through the night."
"– The parlour-door – what stirred it?"
    "– No one: no soul's in range."
"– But, anyhow, I heard it,
        And it seems strange!

"Seek my own room I cannot –
    A figure is on the stair!"
"– What figure?   Nay, I scan not
    Any one lingering there.
A bough outside is waving,
    And that's its shade by the moon."
"– Well, all is strange! I am craving
        Strength to leave soon."

"– Ah, maybe you've some vision
    Of showings beyond our sphere;
Some sight, sense, intuition
    Of what once happened here?
The house is old; they've hinted
    It once held two love-thralls,
And they may have imprinted
        Their dreams on its walls?

"They were – I think 'twas told me –
    Queer in their works and ways;
The teller would often hold me
    With weird tales of those days.
Some folk can not abide here,
    But we – we do not care
Who loved, laughed, wept, or died here,
        Knew joy, or despair."

The Pink Frock

"O my pretty pink frock,
I sha'n't be able to wear it!
Why is he dying just now?
      I can hardly bear it!

"He might have contrived to live on;
But they say there's no hope whatever:
And I must shut myself up,
      And go out never?

"O my pretty pink frock?
Puff-sleeved and accordion-pleated!
He might have passed in July,
      And not so cheated!"

The Choirmaster's Burial

He often would ask us
That, when he died,
After playing so many
To their last rest,
If out of us any
Should here abide,
And it would not task us,
We would with our lutes
Play over him
By his grave-brim
The psalm he liked best –
The one whose sense suits
"Mount Ephraim" –
And perhaps we should seem
To him, in Death's dream,
Like the seraphim.

As soon as I knew
That his spirit was gone
I thought this his due,
And spoke thereupon.
"I think," said the vicar,
"A read service quicker
Than viols out-of-doors
In these frosts and hoars.
That old-fashioned way
Requires a fine day,
And it seems to me
It had better not be."

Hence, that afternoon,
Though never knew he
That his wish could not be,
To get through it faster
They buried the master
Without any tune.

But 'twas said that, when
At the dead of next night
The vicar looked out,
There struck on his ken
Thronged roundabout,
Where the frost was graying
The headstoned grass,
A band all in white
Like the saints in church-glass,
Singing and playing
The ancient stave
By the choirmaster's grave.

Such the tenor man told
When he had grown old.

p. 65: The market town of Shaftesbury, North Dorset.
pp. 66–7: Milton Abbas, East Dorset.
p. 68: Lulworth Castle, East Lulworth, near the Dorset coast.
p. 69: Athelhampton Hall, near Puddletown, at one time a nonconformist school where Tryphena Sparks, Hardy's cousin, was both pupil and teacher.
p. 70: The Lord's Prayer in the parish church of Puddletown, the Hardy family's neighbouring village.
p. 71: Piddlehinton Church, Dorset. Hardy's sister Mary was the schoolmistress in the village.
p. 72: Corfe Castle, East Dorset.

IN ALTISSIMIS DEO GLORIA

Our Father which: wart in heaven. hallowed be thy Name Thy Kingdom come Thy will bedone in earth. as it is in heaven. Give us this day our daily bread. And Forgive us our trespasses as we Forgive them that Trespass against us and lead us not into temptation: But deliver us from evil For thine is the Kingdom, and ye power & the glory For ever & ever. Amen.

Inscriptions for a Peal of Eight Bells

AFTER A RESTORATION

I. Thomas Tremble new-made me
Eighteen hundred and fifty-three:
Why he did I fail to see.

II. I was well-toned by William Brine,
Seventeen hundred and twenty-nine;
Now, re-cast, I weakly whine!

III. Fifteen hundred used to be
My date, but since they melted me
'Tis only eighteen fifty-three.

IV. Henry Hopkins got me made,
And I summon folk as bade;
Not to much purpose, I'm afraid!

V. I likewise; for I bang and bid
In commoner metal than I did,
Some of me being stolen and hid.

VI. I, too, since in a mould they flung me,
Drained my silver, and rehung me,
So that in tin-like tones I tongue me.

VII. In nineteen hundred, so 'tis said,
They cut my canon off my head,
And made me look scalped, scraped, and dead.

VIII. I'm the peal's tenor still, but rue it!
Once it took two to swing me through it:
Now I'm rehung, one dolt can do it.

At The Railway Station, Upway

"There is not much that I can do,
For I've no money that's quite my own!"
Spoke up the pitying child –
A little boy with a violin
At the station before the train came in, –
"But I can play my fiddle to you,
And a nice one 'tis, and good in tone!"

The man in the handcuffs smiled;
The constable looked, and he smiled, too,
    As the fiddle began to twang;
And the man in the handcuffs suddenly sang
            With grimful glee:
            "This life so free
            Is the thing for me!"
And the constable smiled, and said no word,
As if unconscious of what he heard;
And so they went on till the train came in –
The convict, and boy with the violin.

The Lodging-House Fuchsias

Mrs Masters's fuchsias hung
Higher and broader, and brightly swung,
    Bell-like, more and more
Over the narrow garden-path,
Giving the passer a sprinkle-bath
        In the morning.

She put up with their pushful ways,
And made us tenderly lift their sprays,
    Going to her door:
But when her funeral had to pass
They cut back all the flowery mass
        In the morning.

The Little Old Table

Creak, little wood thing, creak,
When I touch you with elbow or knee;
That is the way you speak
Of one who gave you to me!

You, little table, she brought –
Brought me with her own hand,
As she looked at me with a thought
That I did not understand.

– Whoever owns it anon,
And hears it, will never know
What a history hangs upon
This creak from long ago.

Midnight on the Great Western

In the third-class seat sat the journeying boy,
      And the roof-lamp's oily flame
Played down on his listless form and face,
Bewrapt past knowing to what he was going,
      Or whence he came.

In the band of his hat the journeying boy
      Had a ticket stuck; and a string
Around his neck bore the key of his box,
That twinkled gleams of the lamp's sad beams
      Like a living thing.

What past can be yours, O journeying boy
      Towards a world unknown,
Who calmly, as if incurious quite
On all at stake, can undertake
      This plunge alone?

Knows your soul a sphere, O journeying boy,
      Our rude realms far above,
Whence with spacious vision you mark and mete
This region of sin that you find you in,
      But are not of?

The Sunshade

Ah – it's the skeleton of a lady's sunshade,
  Here at my feet in the hard rock's chink,
  Merely a naked sheaf of wires! –
  Twenty years have gone with their livers and diers
  Since it was silked in its white or pink.

Noonshine riddles the ribs of the sunshade,
  No more a screen from the weakest ray;
  Nothing to tell us the hue of its dyes,
  Nothing but rusty bones as it lies
  In its coffin of stone, unseen till to-day.

Where is the woman who carried that sunshade
  Up and down this seaside place? –
  Little thumb standing against its stem,
  Thoughts perhaps bent on a love-stratagem,
  Softening yet more the already soft face!

Is the fair woman who carried that sunshade
　　A skeleton just as her property is,
　　Laid in the chink that none may scan?
　　And does she regret – if regret dust can –
　　The vain things thought when she flourished this?

The Harbour Bridge

From here, the quay, one looks above to mark
The bridge across the harbour, hanging dark
Against the day's-end sky, fair-green in glow
Over and under the middle archway's bow:
It draws its skeleton where the sun has set,
Yea, clear from cutwater to parapet;
On which mild glow, too, lines of rope and spar
　　Trace themselves black as char.

Down here in shade we hear the painters shift
Against the bollards with a drowsy lift,
As moved by the incoming stealthy tide.
High up across the bridge the burghers glide
As cut black-paper portraits hastening on
In conversation none knows what upon:
Their sharp-edged lips move quickly word by word
　　To speech that is not heard.

There trails the dreamful girl, who leans and stops,
There presses the practical woman to the shops,
There is a sailor, meeting his wife with a start,
And we, drawn nearer, judge they are keeping apart.
Both pause.　She says: "I've looked for you.　I thought
We'd make it up."　Then no words can be caught.
At last: "Won't you come home?"　She moves still nigher:
　　"'Tis comfortable, with a fire."

"No," he says gloomily.　"And, anyhow,
I can't give up the other woman now:
You should have talked like that in former days,
When I was last home."　They go different ways.
And the west dims, and yellow lamplights shine:
And soon above, like lamps more opaline,
White stars ghost forth, that care not for men's wives,
　　Or any other lives.
WEYMOUTH

POEMS *1912–13*
Veteris vestigia flammae

The Going

Why did you give no hint that night
That quickly after the morrow's dawn,
And calmly, as if indifferent quite,
You would close your term here, up and be gone
    Where I could not follow
    With wing of swallow
To gain one glimpse of you ever anon!

    Never to bid good-bye,
    Or lip me the softest call,
Or utter a wish for a word, while I
Saw morning harden upon the wall,
    Unmoved, unknowing
    That your great going
Had place that moment, and altered all.

Why do you make me leave the house
And think for a breath it is you I see
At the end of the alley of bending boughs
Where so often at dusk you used to be;
    Till in darkening dankness
    The yawning blankness
Of the perspective sickens me!

    You were she who abode
    By those red-veined rocks far West,
You were the swan-necked one who rode
Along the beetling Beeny Crest,
    And, reining nigh me,
    Would muse and eye me,
While Life unrolled us its very best.

Why, then, latterly did we not speak,
Did we not think of those days long dead,
And ere your vanishing strive to seek
That time's renewal?   We might have said,
    "In this bright spring weather
    We'll visit together
Those places that once we visited."

Well, well! All's past amend,
Unchangeable. It must go.
I seem but a dead man held on end
To sink down soon.... O you could not know
That such swift fleeing
No soul foreseeing –
Not even I – would undo me so!

Your Last Drive

Here by the moorway you returned,
And saw the borough lights ahead
That lit your face – all undiscerned
To be in a week the face of the dead,
And you told of the charm of that haloed view
That never again would beam on you.

And on your left you passed the spot
Where eight days later you were to lie,
And be spoken of as one who was not;
Beholding it with a heedless eye
As alien from you, though under its tree
You soon would halt everlastingly.

I drove not with you.... Yet had I sat
At your side that eve I should not have seen
That the countenance I was glancing at
Had a last-time look in the flickering sheen,
Nor have read the writing upon your face,
"I go hence soon to my resting-place;

"You may miss me then. But I shall not know
How many times you visit me there,
Or what your thoughts are, or if you go
There never at all. And I shall not care.
Should you censure me I shall take no heed,
And even your praises no more shall need."

True: never you'll know. And you will not mind
But shall I then slight you because of such?
Dear ghost, in the past did you ever find
The thought "What profit," move me much?
Yet abides the fact, indeed, the same, –
You are past love, praise, indifference, blame.

The Walk

You did not walk with me
Of late to the hill-top tree
    By the gated ways,
    As in earlier days;
    You were weak and lame,
    So you never came,
And I went alone, and I did not mind,
Not thinking of you as left behind.

I walked up there to-day
Just in the former way;
    Surveyed around
    The familiar ground
    By myself again:
    What difference, then?
Only that underlying sense
Of the look of a room on returning thence.

"I Found Her Out There"

I found her out there
On a slope few see,
That falls westwardly
To the salt-edged air,
Where the ocean breaks
On the purple strand,
And the hurricane shakes
The solid land.

I brought her here,
And have laid her to rest
In a noiseless nest
No sea beats near.
She will never be stirred
In her loamy cell
By the waves long heard
And loved so well.

So she does not sleep
By those haunted heights
The Atlantic smites
And the blind gales sweep,
Whence she often would gaze
At Dundagel's famed head,
While the dipping blaze
Dyed her face fire-red;

And would sigh at the tale
Of sunk Lyonnesse,
As a wind-tugged tress
Flapped her cheek like a flail;
Or listen at whiles
With a thought-bound brow
To the murmuring miles
She is far from now.

Yet her shade, maybe,
Will creep underground
Till it catch the sound
Of that western sea
As it swells and sobs
Where she once domiciled,
And joy in its throbs
With the heart of a child.

Without Ceremony

It was your way, my dear,
To vanish without a word
When callers, friends, or kin
Had left, and I hastened in
To rejoin you, as I inferred.

And when you'd a mind to career
Off anywhere – say to town –
You were all on a sudden gone
Before I had thought thereon,
Or noticed your trunks were down.

So, now that you disappear
For ever in that swift style,
Your meaning seems to me
Just as it used to be:
"Good-bye is not worth while!"

The Haunter

He does not think that I haunt here nightly:
 How shall I let him know
That whither his fancy sets him wandering
 I, too, alertly go? –
Hover and hover a few feet from him
 Just as I used to do,
But cannot answer the words he lifts me –
 Only listen thereto!

When I could answer he did not say them:
 When I could let him know
How I would like to join in his journeys
 Seldom he wished to go.
Now that he goes and wants me with him
 More than he used to do,
Never he sees my faithful phantom
 Though he speaks thereto.

Yes, I companion him to places
 Only dreamers know,
Where the shy hares print long paces,
 Where the night rooks go;
Into old aisles where the past is all to him,
 Close as his shade can do,
Always lacking the power to call to him,
 Near as I reach thereto!

What a good haunter I am, O tell him!
 Quickly make him know
If he but sigh since my loss befell him
 Straight to his side I go.
Tell him a faithful one is doing
 All that love can do
Still that his path may be worth pursuing,
 And to bring peace thereto.

The Voice

Woman much missed, how you call to me, call to me,
Saying that now you are not as you were
When you had changed from the one who was all to me,
But as at first, when our day was fair.

Can it be you that I hear?   Let me view you, then,
Standing as when I drew near to the town
Where you would wait for me: yes, as I knew you then,
Even to the original air-blue gown!

Or is it only the breeze, in its listlessness
Travelling across the wet mead to me here,
You being ever dissolved to wan wistlessness,
Heard no more again far or near?

Thus I; faltering forward,
Leaves around me falling,
Wind oozing thin through the thorn from norward,
And the woman calling.

A Dream or No

Why go to Saint-Juliot?   What's Juliot to me?
Some strange necromancy
But charmed me to fancy
That much of my life claims the spot as its key.

Yes.   I have had dreams of that place in the West,
And a maiden abiding
Thereat as in hiding;
Fair-eyed and white-shouldered, broad-browed and brown-tressed.

And of how, coastward bound on a night long ago,
There lonely I found her,
The sea-birds around her,
And other than nigh things uncaring to know.

So sweet her life there (in my thought has it seemed)
That quickly she drew me
To take her unto me,
And lodge her long years with me.   Such have I dreamed.

But nought of that maid from Saint-Juliot I see;
Can she ever have been here,
And shed her life's sheen here,
The woman I thought a long housemate with me?

Does there even a place like Saint-Juliot exist?
Or a Vallency Valley
With stream and leafed alley,
Or Beeny, or Bos with its flounce flinging mist?

After a Journey

Hereto I come to view a voiceless ghost;
   Whither, O whither will its whim now draw me?
Up the cliff, down, till I'm lonely, lost,
   And the unseen water's ejaculations awe me.
Where you will next be there's no knowing,
    Facing round about me everywhere,
       With your nut-coloured hair,
And gray eyes, and rose-flush coming and going.

Yes: I have re-entered your olden haunts at last;
   Through the years, through the dead scenes I have tracked you;
What have you now found to say of our past –
   Scanned across the dark space wherein I have lacked you?
Summer gave us sweets, but autumn wrought division?
    Things were not lastly as firstly well
       With us twain, you tell?
But all's closed now, despite Time's derision.

I see what you are doing: you are leading me on
   To the spots we knew when we haunted here together,
The waterfall, above which the mist-bow shone
   At the then fair hour in the then fair weather,
And the cave just under, with a voice still so hollow
    That it seems to call out to me from forty years ago,
       When you were all aglow,
And not the thin ghost that I now frailly follow!

Ignorant of what there is flitting here to see,
   The waked birds preen and the seals flop lazily;
Soon you will have, Dear, to vanish from me,
   For the stars close their shutters and the dawn whitens hazily.
Trust me, I mind not, though Life lours,
    The bringing me here; nay, bring me here again!
       I am just the same as when
Our days were a joy, and our paths through flowers.

    PENTARGAN BAY

Beeny Cliff

MARCH 1870–MARCH 1913

I

O the opal and the sapphire of that wandering western sea,
And the woman riding high above with bright hair flapping free –
The woman whom I loved so, and who loyally loved me.

II

The pale mews plained below us, and the waves seemed far away
In a nether sky, engrossed in saying their ceaseless babbling say,
As we laughed light-heartedly aloft on that clear-sunned March day.

III

A little cloud then cloaked us, and there flew an irised rain,
And the Atlantic dyed its levels with a dull misfeatured stain,
And then the sun burst out again, and purples prinked the main.

IV

– Still in all its chasmal beauty bulks old Beeny to the sky,
And shall she and I not go there once again now March is nigh,
And the sweet things said in that March say anew there by and by?

V

What if still in chasmal beauty looms that wild weird western shore,
The woman now is – elsewhere – whom the ambling pony bore,
And not knows nor cares for Beeny, and will laugh there never more.

At Castle Boterel

As I drive to the junction of lane and highway,
    And the drizzle bedrenches the waggonette,
I look behind at the fading byway,
    And see on its slope, now glistening wet,
        Distinctly yet

Myself and a girlish form benighted
    In dry March weather.   We climb the road
Beside a chaise.   We had just alighted
    To ease the sturdy pony's load
        When he sighed and slowed.

What we did as we climbed, and what we talked of
    Matters not much, nor to what it led, –
Something that life will not be balked of
    Without rude reason till hope is dead,
        And feeling fled.

It filled but a minute.   But was there ever
    A time of such quality, since or before,
In that hill's story?   To one mind never,
    Though it has been climbed, foot-swift, foot-sore,
        By thousands more.

Primaeval rocks form the road's steep border,
    And much have they faced there, first and last,
Of the transitory in Earth's long order;
    But what they record in colour and cast
        Is – that we two passed.

And to me, though Time's unflinching rigour,
    In mindless rote, has ruled from sight
The substance now, one phantom figure
    Remains on the slope, as when that night
        Saw us alight.

I look and see it there, shrinking, shrinking,
    I look back at it amid the rain
For the very last time; for my sand is sinking,
    And I shall traverse old love's domain
        Never again.

The Marble-Streeted Town

I reach the marble-streeted town,
    Whose "Sound" outbreathes its air
      Of sharp sea-salts;
I see the movement up and down
    As when she was there.
Ships of all countries come and go,
    The bandsmen boom in the sun
      A throbbing waltz;
The schoolgirls laugh along the Hoe
    As when she was one.

I move away as the music rolls:
    The place seems not to mind
      That she – of old
The brightest of its native souls –
      Left it behind!
Over this green aforedays she
    On light treads went and came.
      Yea, times untold;
Yet none here knows her history –
      Has heard her name.

PLYMOUTH

"She Opened the Door"

She opened the door of the West to me,
    With its loud sea-lashings,
    And cliff-side clashings
Of waters rife with revelry.

She opened the door of Romance to me,
    The door from a cell
    I had known too well,
Too long, till then, and was fain to flee.

She opened the door of a Love to me,
    That passed the wry
    World-welters by
As far as the arching blue the lea.

She opens the door of the Past to me,
    Its magic lights,
    Its heavenly heights,
When forward little is to see!

WAR POEMS, POEMS ON PUBLIC THEMES, COMEDIES,
LAMENTS AND FAREWELLS

Drummer Hodge

I

They throw in Drummer Hodge, to rest
    Uncoffined – just as found:
His landmark is a kopje-crest
    That breaks the veldt around;
And foreign constellations west
    Each night above his mound.

II

Young Hodge the Drummer never knew –
    Fresh from his Wessex home –
The meaning of the broad Karoo,
    The Bush, the dusty loam,
And why uprose to nightly view
    Strange stars amid the gloam.

III

Yet portion of that unknown plain
    Will Hodge for ever be;
His homely Northern breast and brain
    Grow to some Southern tree,
And strange-eyed constellations reign
    His stars eternally.

A New Year's Eve in War Time

I

Phantasmal fears,
And the flap of the flame,
And the throb of the clock,
And a loosened slate,
And the blind night's drone,
Which tiredly the spectral pines intone!

II

And the blood in my ears
Strumming always the same,
And the gable-cock
With its fitful grate,
And myself, alone.

III

The twelfth hour nears
Hand-hid, as in shame;
I undo the lock,
And listen, and wait
For the Young Unknown.

IV

In the dark there careers –
As if Death astride came
To numb all with his knock –
A horse at mad rate
Over rut and stone.

V

No figure appears,
No call of my name,
No sound but "Tic-toc"
Without check.   Past the gate
It clatters – is gone.

VI

What rider it bears
There is none to proclaim;
And the Old Year has struck,
And, scarce animate.
The New makes moan.

VII

Maybe that "More Tears! –
More Famine and Flame –
More Severance and Shock!"
Is the order from Fate
That the Rider speeds on
To pale Europe; and tiredly the pines intone.

p. 89: Marshlands near Salisbury, Wiltshire.
pp. 90–1: Washing in a Dorset garden.
p. 92: A country home in Dorset.
p. 93: A stone wall on Salisbury Plain.
pp. 94–5: Early morning near Chideock, Western Dorset.
p. 96: The Neolithic giant carved in the chalk hillside at Cerne Abbas, mid-Dorset.

In Time of "The Breaking of Nations"

I

Only a man harrowing clods
   In a slow silent walk
With an old horse that stumbles and nods
   Half asleep as they stalk.

II

Only thin smoke without flame
   From the heaps of couch-grass;
Yet this will go onward the same
   Though Dynasties pass.

III

Yonder a maid and her wight
   Come whispering by:
War's annals will cloud into night
   Ere their story die.

Channel Firing

That night your great guns, unawares,
Shook all our coffins as we lay,
And broke the chancel window-squares,
We thought it was the Judgment-day

And sat upright. While drearisome
Arose the howl of wakened hounds:
The mouse let fall the altar-crumb,
The worms drew back into the mounds,

The glebe cow drooled. Till God called, "No:
It's gunnery practice out at sea
Just as before you went below;
The world is as it used to be:

"All nations striving strong to make
Red war yet redder. Mad as hatters
They do no more for Christés sake
Than you who are helpless in such matters.

"That this is not the judgment-hour
For some of them's a blessed thing,
For if it were they'd have to scour
Hell's floor for so much threatening....

"Ha, ha. It will be warmer when
I blow the trumpet (if indeed
I ever do; for you are men,
And rest eternal sorely need)."

So down we lay again. "I wonder,
Will the world ever saner be,"
Said one, "than when He sent us under
In our indifferent century!"

And many a skeleton shook his head.
"Instead of preaching forty year,"
My neighbour Parson Thirdly said,
"I wish I had stuck to pipes and beer."

Again, the guns disturbed the hour,
Roaring their readiness to avenge,
As far inland as Stourton Tower,
And Camelot, and starlit Stonehenge.

The Convergence of the Twain

(LINES ON THE LOSS OF THE *Titanic*)

I

In a solitude of the sea
Deep from human vanity,
And the Pride of Life that planned her, stilly couches she.

II

Steel chambers, late the pyres
Of her salamandrine fires,
Cold currents thrid, and turn to rhythmic tidal lyres.

III

Over the mirrors meant
To glass the opulent
The sea-worm crawls - grotesque, slimed, dumb, indifferent.

IV

Jewels in joy designed
To ravish the sensuous mind
Lie lightless, all their sparkles bleared and black and blind.

V

Dim moon-eyed fishes near
Gaze at the gilded gear
And query: "What does this vaingloriousness down here?"

VI

Well: while was fashioning
This creature of cleaving wing,
The Immanent Will that stirs and urges everything

VII

Prepared a sinister mate
For her – so gaily great –
A Shape of Ice, for the time far and dissociate.

VIII

And as the smart ship grew
In stature, grace, and hue,
In shadowy silent distance grew the Iceberg too.

IX

Alien they seemed to be:
No mortal eye could see
The intimate welding of their later history,

X

Or sign that they were bent
By paths coincident
On being anon twin halves of one august event.

XI

Till the Spinner of the Years
Said "Now!"   And each one hears,
And consummation comes, and jars two hemispheres.

"And There Was a Great Calm"

(ON THE SIGNING OF THE ARMISTICE, NOV. 11, 1918)

I

There had been years of Passion – scorching, cold,
And much Despair, and Anger heaving high,
Care whitely watching, Sorrows manifold,
Among the young, among the weak and old,
And the pensive Spirit of Pity whispered, "Why?"

II

Men had not paused to answer.   Foes distraught
Pierced the thinned peoples in a brute-like blindness,
Philosophies that sages long had taught,
And Selflessness, were as an unknown thought,
And "Hell!" and "Shell!" were yapped at Lovingkindness.

III

The feeble folk at home had grown full-used
To "dug-outs," "snipers," "Huns," from the war-adept
In the mornings heard, and at evetides perused;
To day-dreamt men in millions, when they mused –
To nightmare-men in millions when they slept.

IV

Waking to wish existence timeless, null,
Sirius they watched above where armies fell;
He seemed to check his flapping when, in the lull
Of night a boom came thencewise, like the dull
Plunge of a stone dropped into some deep well.

V

So, when old hopes that earth was bettering slowly
Were dead and damned, there sounded "War is done!"
One morrow.   Said the bereft, and meek, and lowly,
"Will men some day be given to grace? yea, wholly,
And in good sooth, as our dreams used to run?"

VI

Breathless they paused.   Out there men raised their glance
To where had stood those poplars lank and lopped,
As they had raised it through the four years' dance
Of Death in the now familiar flats of France;
And murmured, "Strange, this!   How?   All firing stopped?"

VII

Aye; all was hushed.   The about-to-fire fired not,
The aimed-at moved away in trance-lipped song.
One checkless regiment slung a clinching shot
And turned.   The Spirit of Irony smirked out, "What?
Spoil peradventures woven of Rage and Wrong?"

VIII

Thenceforth no flying fires inflamed the gray,
No hurtlings shook the dewdrop from the thorn,
No moan perplexed the mute bird on the spray;
Worn horses mused: "We are not whipped to-day";
No weft-winged engines blurred the moon's thin horn.

IX

Calm fell.   From Heaven distilled a clemency;
There was peace on earth, and silence in the sky;
Some could, some could not, shake off misery:
The Sinister Spirit sneered: "It had to be!"
And again the Spirit of Pity whispered, "Why?"

An Ancient to Ancients

Where once we danced, where once we sang,.
        Gentlemen,
The floors are sunken, cobwebs hang,
And cracks creep; worms have fed upon
The doors.   Yea, sprightlier times were then
Than now, with harps and tabrets gone,
        Gentlemen!

Where once we rowed, where once we sailed
        Gentlemen,
And damsels took the tiller, veiled
Against too strong a stare (God wot
Their fancy, then or anywhen!)
Upon that shore we are clean forgot,
        Gentlemen!

We have lost somewhat, afar and near,
        Gentlemen,
The thinning of our ranks each year
Affords a hint we are nigh undone,
That we shall not be ever again
The marked of many, loved of one,
        Gentlemen.

In dance the polka hit our wish,
     Gentlemen,
The paced quadrille, the spry schottische,
"Sir Roger." – And in opera spheres
The "Girl" (the famed "Bohemian"),
And "Trovatore," held the ears,
     Gentlemen.

This season's paintings do not please,
     Gentlemen,
Like Etty, Mulready, Maclise;
Throbbing romance has waned and wanned;
No wizard wields the witching pen
Of Bulwer, Scott, Dumas, and Sand,
     Gentlemen.

The bower we shrined to Tennyson,
     Gentlemen,
Is roof-wrecked; damps there drip upon
Sagged seats, the creeper-nails are rust,
The spider is sole denizen;
Even she who voiced those rhymes is dust,
     Gentlemen!

We who met sunrise sanguine-souled,
     Gentlemen,
Are wearing weary.   We are old;
These younger press; we feel our rout
Is imminent to Aïdes' den, –
That evening shades are stretching out,
     Gentlemen!

And yet, though ours be failing frames,
     Gentlemen,
So were some others' history names,
Who trode their track light-limbed and fast
As these youth, and not alien
From enterprise, to their long last,
     Gentlemen.

Sophocles, Plato, Socrates,
     Gentlemen,
Pythagoras, Thucydides,
Herodotus, and Homer, – yea,
Clement, Augustin, Origen,
Burnt brightlier towards their setting-day,
     Gentlemen.

And ye, red-lipped and smooth-browed; list,
   Gentlemen;
Much is there waits you we have missed;
Much lore we leave you worth the knowing,
Much, much has lain outside our ken:
Nay, rush not: time serves: we are going,
   Gentlemen.

The Ruined Maid

"O 'melia, my dear, this does everything crown!
Who could have supposed I should meet you in Town?
And whence such fair garments, such prosperi-ty?" –
"O didn't you know I'd been ruined?" said she.

– "You left us in tatters, without shoes or socks,
Tired of digging potatoes, and spudding up docks;
And now you've gay bracelets and bright feathers three!" –
"Yes: that's how we dress when we're ruined," said she.

– "At home in the barton you said 'thee' and 'thou,'
And 'thik oon,' and 'theäs oon,' and 't'other'; but now
Your talking quite fits 'ee for high compa-ny!" –
"Some polish is gained with one's ruin," said she.

– "Your hands were like paws then, your face blue and bleak
But now I'm bewitched by your delicate cheek,
And your little gloves fit as on any la-dy!" –
"We never do work when we're ruined," said she.

– "You used to call home-life a hag-ridden dream,
And you'd sigh, and you'd sock; but at present you seem
To know not of megrims or melancho-ly!" –
"True. One's pretty lively when ruined," said she.

– "I wish I had feathers, a fine sweeping gown,
And a delicate face, and could strut about Town!" –
"My dear – a raw country girl, such as you be,
Cannot quite expect that. You ain't ruined," said she.

The Self-Unseeing

Here is the ancient floor,
Footworn and hollowed and thin,
Here was the former door
Where the dead feet walked in.

She sat here in her chair,
Smiling into the fire;
He who played stood there,
Bowing it higher and higher.

Childlike, I danced in a dream;
Blessings emblazoned that day;
Everything glowed with a gleam;
Yet we were looking away!

"I Look Into My Glass"

I look into my glass,
And view my wasting skin,
And say, "Would God it came to pass
My heart had shrunk as thin!"

For then, I, undistrest
By hearts grown cold to me,
Could lonely wait my endless rest
With equanimity.

But Time, to make me grieve,
Part steals, lets part abide;
And shakes this fragile frame at eve
With throbbings of noontide.

Heredity

I am the family face;
Flesh perishes, I live on,
Projecting trait and trace
Through time to times anon,
And leaping from place to place
Over oblivion.

The years-heired feature that can
In curve and voice and eye
Despise the human span
Of durance – that is I;
The eternal thing in man,
That heeds no call to die.

The Darkling Thrush

I leant upon a coppice gate
    When Frost was spectre-gray,
And Winter's dregs made desolate
    The weakening eye of day.
The tangled bine-stems scored the sky
    Like strings of broken lyres,
And all mankind that haunted nigh
    Had sought their household fires.

The land's sharp features seemed to be
    The Century's corpse outleant,
His crypt the cloudy canopy,
    The wind his death-lament.
The ancient pulse of germ and birth
    Was shrunken hard and dry,
And every spirit upon earth
    Seemed fervourless as I.

At once a voice arose among
    The bleak twigs overhead
In a full-hearted evensong
    Of joy illimited;
An aged thrush, frail, gaunt, and small,
    In blast-beruffled plume,
Had chosen thus to fling his soul
    Upon the growing gloom.

So little cause for carolings
    Of such ecstatic sound
Was written on terrestrial things
    Afar or nigh around,
That I could think there trembled through
    His happy good-night air
Some blessed Hope, whereof he knew
    And I was unaware.

Evening Shadows

The shadows of my chimneys stretch afar
Across the plot, and on to the privet bower,
And even the shadows of their smokings show,
And nothing says just now that where they are
They will in future stretch at this same hour,
Though in my earthen cyst I shall not know.

And at this time the neighbouring Pagan mound,
Whose myths the Gospel news now supersede,
Upon the greensward also throws its shade,
And nothing says such shade will spread around
Even as to-day when men will no more heed
The Gospel news than when the mound was made.

Silences

There is the silence of a copse or croft
      When the wind sinks dumb,
      And of a belfry-loft
When the tenor after tolling stops its hum.

And there's the silence of a lonely pond
      Where a man was drowned,
      Nor nigh nor yond
A newt, frog, toad, to make the merest sound.

But the rapt silence of an empty house
      Where oneself was born,
      Dwelt, held carouse
With friends, is of all silences most forlorn!

Past are remembered songs and music-strains
      Once audible there:
      Roof, rafters, panes
Look absent-thoughted, tranced, or locked in prayer.

It seems no power on earth can waken it
      Or rouse its rooms,
      Or its past permit
The present to stir a torpor like a tomb's.

On the Tune Called
The Old-Hundred-And-Fourth

We never sang together
   Ravenscroft's terse old tune
On Sundays or on weekdays,
In sharp or summer weather,
   At night-time or at noon.

Why did we never sing it,
   Why never so incline
On Sundays or on weekdays,
Even when soft wafts would wing it
   From your far floor to mine?

Shall we that tune, then, never
   Stand voicing side by side
On Sundays or on weekdays? ...
Or shall we, when for ever
   In Sheol we abide,

Sing it in desolation,
   As we might long have done
On Sundays or on weekdays
With love and exultation
   Before our sands had run?

Lines

TO A MOVEMENT IN MOZART'S E-FLAT SYMPHONY

Show me again the time
   When in the Junetide's prime
We flew by meads and mountains northerly! –
Yea, to such freshness, fairness, fulness, fineness, freeness,
   Love lures life on.

Show me again the day
   When from the sandy bay
We looked together upon the pestered sea! –
Yea, to such surging, swaying, sighing, swelling, shrinking,
   Love lures life on.

Show me again the hour
When by the pinnacled tower
We eyed each other and feared futurity! –
Yea, to such bodings, broodings, beatings, blanchings, blessings,
Love lures life on.

Show me again just this:
The moment of that kiss
Away from the prancing folk, by the strawberry-tree! –
Yea, to such rashness, ratheness, rareness, ripeness, richness,
Loves lures life on.

Mismet

I

He was leaning by a face,
He was looking into eyes,
And he knew a trysting-place,
And he heard seductive sighs;
But the face,
And the eyes,
And the place,
And the sighs,
Were not, alas, the right ones – the ones meet for him –
Though fine and sweet the features, and the feelings all abrim.

II

She was looking at a form,
She was listening for a tread,
She could feel a waft of charm
When a certain name was said;
But the form,
And the tread,
And the charm,
And name said,
Were the wrong ones for her, and ever would be so,
While the heritor of the right it would have saved her soul to know!

In Tenebris

I

"Percussus sum sicut foenum, et aruit cor meum." – *Ps.* CI

Wintertime nighs;
But my bereavement-pain
It cannot bring again:
    Twice no one dies.

Flower-petals flee;
But, since it once hath been,
No more that severing scene
    Can harrow me.

Birds faint in dread:
I shall not lose old strength
In the lone frost's black length:
    Strength long since fled!

Leaves freeze to dun;
But friends can not turn cold
This season as of old
    For him with none.

Tempests may scath;
But love can not make smart
Again this year his heart
    Who no heart hath.

Black is night's cope;
But death will not appal
One who, past doubtings all,
    Waits in unhope.

In Tenebris

II

"Considerabam ad dexteram, et videbam; et non erat qui cognosceret me.... Non est qui requirat animam meam." – *Ps.* CXLI

When the clouds' swoln bosoms echo back the shouts of the many and strong
That things are all as they best may be, save a few to be right ere long,
And my eyes have not the vision in them to discern what to these is so clear,
The blot seems straightway in me alone; one better he were not here.

The stout upstanders say, All's well with us: ruers have nought to rue!
And what the potent say so oft, can it fail to be somewhat true?
Breezily go they, breezily come; their dust smokes around their career,
Till I think I am one born out of due time, who has no calling here.

Their dawns bring lusty joys, it seems; their evenings all that is sweet;
Our times are blessed times, they cry: Life shapes it as is most meet,
And nothing is much the matter; there are many smiles to a tear;
Then what is the matter is I, I say.   Why should such an one be here? ....

Let him in whose ears the low-voiced Best is killed by the clash of the First,
Who holds that if way to the Better there be, it exacts a full look at the Worst,
Who feels that delight is a delicate growth cramped by crookedness, custom, and fear,
Get him up and be gone as one shaped awry; he disturbs the order here.

In Tenebris

III

*"Heu mihi, quia incolatus meus prolongatus est!   Habitavi cum habitantibus Cedar; multum
incola fuit anima mea." - Ps. cxix*

There have been times when I well might have passed and the ending have come –
Points in my path when the dark might have stolen on me, artless, unrueing –
Ere I had learnt that the world was a welter of futile doing:
Such had been times when I well might have passed, and the ending have come!

Say, on the noon when the half-sunny hours told that April was nigh,
And I upgathered and cast forth the snow from the crocus-border,
Fashioned and furbished the soil into a summer-seeming order,
Glowing in gladsome faith that I quickened the year thereby.

Or on that loneliest of eves when afar and benighted we stood,
She who upheld me and I, in the midmost of Egdon together,
Confident I in her watching and ward through the blackening heather,
Deeming her matchless in might and with measureless scope endued.

Or on that winter-wild night when, reclined by the chimney-nook quoin,
Slowly a drowse overgat me, the smallest and feeblest of folk there,
Weak from my baptism of pain; when at times and anon I awoke there –
Heard of a world wheeling on, with no listing or longing to join.

Even then! while unweeting that vision could vex or that knowledge could numb,
That sweets to the mouth in the belly are bitter, and tart, and untoward,
Then, on some dim-coloured scene should my briefly raised curtain have lowered,
Then might the Voice that is law have said "Cease!" and the ending have come.

Intra Sepulchrum

What curious things we said,
What curious things we did
Up there in the world we walked till dead,
Our kith and kin amid!

How we played at love,
And its wildness, weakness, woe;
Yes, played thereat far more than enough
As it turned out, I trow!

Played at believing in gods
And observing the ordinances,
I for your sake in impossible codes
Right ready to acquiesce.

Thinking our lives unique,
Quite quainter than usual kinds,
We held that we could not abide a week
The tether of typic minds.

– Yet people who day by day
Pass by and look at us
From over the wall in a casual way
Are of this unconscious.

And feel, if anything,
That none can be buried here
Removed from commonest fashioning,
Or lending note to a bier:

No twain who in heart-heaves proved
Themselves at all adept,
Who more than many laughed and loved
Who more than many wept,

Or were as sprites or elves
Into blind matter hurled,
Or ever could have been to themselves
The centre of the world.

Mute Opinion

I

I traversed a dominion
Whose spokesmen spake out strong
Their purpose and opinion
Through pulpit, press, and song.
I scarce had means to note there
A large-eyed few, and dumb,
Who thought not as those thought there
That stirred the heat and hum.

II

When, grown a Shade, beholding
That land in lifetime trode,
To learn if its unfolding
Fulfilled its clamoured code,
I saw, in web unbroken,
Its history outwrought
Not as the loud had spoken,
But as the mute had thought.

p. 113: Thomas Hardy aged 35 and his first wife, Emma, aged about 30.
p. 114: A St Juliot farmer returning from milking. St Juliot's Church, North Cornwall (background), was the meeting-place of Thomas and Emma in their courting days.
p. 115: St Juliot: a corner of a farmyard, with farmyard cat.
p. 116: Water-mill at Boscastle, North Cornwall, the 'Castle Boterel' of Hardy's 1912–13 sequence of poems recalling his courtship of Emma.
p. 117: Roche Rock, on the high downs near St Austell.
p. 118: Near Tintagel, on the Atlantic coast of Cornwall.
p. 119: '... much have they faced there, first and last,
      Of the transitory Earth's long order ...'

Boscastle harbour in Hardy's poem, 'At Castle Boterel'.
p. 120: A Cornish lane.

Before Life and After

A time there was – as one may guess
And as, indeed, earth's testimonies tell. –
Before the birth of consciousness,
    When all went well.

None suffered sickness, love, or loss,
None knew regret, starved hope, or heart-burnings;
None cared whatever crash or cross
    Brought wrack to things.

If something ceased, no tongue bewailed,
If something winced and waned, no heart was wrung;
If brightness dimmed, and dark prevailed,
    No sense was stung.

But the disease of feeling germed,
And primal rightness took the tinct of wrong;
Ere nescience shall be reaffirmed
    How long, how long?

The Last Signal

(OCT. 11, 1886)

A MEMORY OF WILLIAM BARNES

Silently I footed by an uphill road
That led from my abode to a spot yew-boughed;
Yellowly the sun sloped low down to westward,
    And dark was the east with cloud.

Then, amid the shadow of that livid sad east,
  Where the light was least, and a gate stood wide,
Something flashed the fire of the sun that was facing it,
    Like a brief blaze on that side.

Looking hard and harder I knew what it meant –
The sudden shine sent from the livid east scene;
It meant the west mirrored by the coffin of my friend there,
    Turning to the road from his green,

To take his last journey forth – he who in his prime
  Trudged so many a time from that gate athwart the land!
Thus a farewell to me he signalled on his grave-way,
    As with a wave of his hand.

Afterwards

When the Present has latched its postern behind my tremulous stay,
    And the May month flaps its glad green leaves like wings,
Delicate-filmed as new-spun silk, will the neighbours say,
    "He was a man who used to notice such things"?

If it be in the dusk when, like an eyelid's soundless blink,
    The dewfall-hawk comes crossing the shades to alight
Upon the wind-warped upland thorn, a gazer may think,
    "To him this must have been a familiar sight."

If I pass during some nocturnal blackness, mothy and warm,
    When the hedgehog travels furtively over the lawn,
One may say, "He strove that such innocent creatures should come to no harm,
    But he could do little for them; and now he is gone."

If, when hearing that I have been stilled at last, they stand at the door,
    Watching the full-starred heavens that winter sees,
Will this thought rise on those who will meet my face no more,
    "He was one who had an eye for such mysteries"?

And will any say when my bell of quittance is heard in the gloom,
    And a crossing breeze cuts a pause in its outrollings,
Till they rise again, as they were a new bell's boom,
    "He hears it not now, but used to notice such things"?

The Aged Newspaper Soliloquizes

Yes; yes; I am old.   In me appears
The history of a hundred years;
Empires', kings', captives', births and deaths,
Strange faiths, and fleeting shibboleths.
– Tragedy, comedy, throngs my page
Beyond all mummed on any stage:
Cold hearts beat hot, hot hearts beat cold,
And I beat on.   Yes; yes; I am old.

He Never Expected Much

or

A CONSIDERATION

(A REFLECTION) ON MY EIGHTY-SIXTH BIRTHDAY

Well, World, you have kept faith with me,
    Kept faith with me;
Upon the whole you have proved to be
    Much as you said you were.
Since as a child I used to lie
Upon the leaze and watch the sky,
Never, I own, expected I
    That life would all be fair.

'Twas then you said, and since have said,
    Times since have said,
In that mysterious voice you shed
    From clouds and hills around:
"Many have loved me desperately,
Many with smooth serenity,
While some have shown contempt of me
    Till they dropped underground.

"I do not promise overmuch,
    Child; overmuch;
Just neutral-tinted haps and such,"
    You said to minds like mine.
Wise warning for your credit's sake!
Which I for one failed not to take,
And hence could stem such strain and ache
    As each year might assign.

Christmas: 1924

"Peace upon earth!" was said.   We sing it,
And pay a million priests to bring it.
After two thousand years of mass
We've got as far as poison-gas.

Christmas in the Elgin Room

BRITISH MUSEUM: EARLY LAST CENTURY

"What is the noise that shakes the night,
  And seems to soar to the Pole-star height?"
    – "Christmas bells,
    The watchman tells
Who walks this hall that blears us captives with its blight."

"And what, then, mean such clangs, so clear?"
" – 'Tis said to have been a day of cheer,
    And source of grace
    To the human race
Long ere their woven sails winged us to exile here.

"We are those whom Christmas overthrew
Some centuries after Pheidias knew
    How to shape us
    And bedrape us
And to set us in Athena's temple for men's view.

"O it is sad now we are sold –
We gods! for Borean people's gold,
    And brought to the gloom
    Of this gaunt room
Which sunlight shuns, and sweet Aurore but enters cold.

"For all these bells, would I were still
Radiant as on Athenai's Hill."
    – "And I, and I!"
    The others sigh,
"Before this Christ was known, and we had men's good will."

Thereat old Helios could but nod,
Throbbed, too, the Ilissus River-god,
    And the torsos there
    Of deities fair,
Whose limbs were shards beneath some Acropolitan clod.

Demeter too, Poseidon hoar,
Persephone, and many more
    Of Zeus' high breed, –
    All loth to heed
What the bells sang that night which shook them to the core.

A Necessitarian's Epitaph

A world I did not wish to enter
Took me and poised me on my centre,
Made me grimace, and foot, and prance,
As cats on hot bricks have to dance
Strange jigs to keep them from the floor,
Till they sink down and feel no more.

A Private Man on Public Men

When my contemporaries were driving
Their coach through Life with strain and striving,
And raking riches into heaps,
And ably pleading in the Courts
With smart rejoinders and retorts,
Or where the Senate nightly keeps
Its vigils, till their fames were fanned
By rumour's tongue throughout the land,
I lived in quiet, screened, unknown,
Pondering upon some stick or stone,
Or news of some rare book or bird
Latterly bought, or seen, or heard,
Not wishing ever to set eyes on
The surging crowd beyond the horizon,
Tasting years of moderate gladness
Mellowed by sundry days of sadness,
Shut from the noise of the world without,
Hearing but dimly its rush and rout,
Unenvying those amid its roar,
Little endowed, not wanting more.

"We are Getting to the End"

We are getting to the end of visioning
The impossible within this universe,
Such as that better whiles may follow worse,
And that our race may mend by reasoning.

We know that even as larks in cages sing
Unthoughtful of deliverance from the curse
That holds them lifelong in a latticed hearse,
We ply spasmodically our pleasuring.

And that when nations set them to lay waste
Their neighbours' heritage by foot and horse,
And hack their pleasant plains in festering seams,
They may again, – not warely, or from taste,
But tickled mad by some demonic force. –
Yes.   We are getting to the end of dreams!

He Resolves to Say No More

O my soul, keep the rest unknown!
It is too like a sound of moan
　　　　When the charnel-eyed
　　　　Pale Horse has nighed:
Yea, none shall gather what I hide!

Why load men's minds with more to bear
That bear already ails to spare?
　　　　From now alway
　　　　Till my last day
What I discern I will not say.

Let Time roll backward if it will;
(Magians who drive the midnight quill
　　　　With brain aglow
　　　　Can see it so,)
What I have learnt no man shall know.

And if my vision range beyond
The blinkered sight of souls in bond,
　　　　– By truth made free –
　　　　I'll let all be,
And show to no man what I see.

Chronology

1839 December: Thomas Hardy's father, self-employed mason and bricklayer, marries Jemima Hand, at Melbury Osmond, Dorset.

1840 2 June: Thomas Hardy, the first of the Hardys' four children, born at Higher Bockhampton, Stinsford, Dorset.

1848 Thomas Hardy attends village school; two years later he moves to a day school in Dorchester.

1856 He is taken on as an apprentice to a Dorchester architect, John Hicks.

1857 Meets Henry Moule, his great friend and mentor. Writes his first poem.

1862 Goes to London where he lodges in Kilburn. Starts job as a Gothic draughtsman, church restorer and designer.

1863 Moves to lodgings at Westbourne Park Villas, London, where he starts writing poetry in earnest.

1867 Returns to Higher Bockhampton and works again for John Hicks.

1868 Completes his first novel, which is not published.

1869 Lives and works for a short while in Weymouth, where he may have had a serious love affair with his cousin Tryphena.

1870 March: Visits St Juliot, near Boscastle in Cornwall, and meets Emma Lavinia Gifford.

1871-3 Publication of his novel *Desperate Remedies*, followed by publication of *Under the Greenwood Tree* and *A Pair of Blue Eyes* and serialisation of *Far From the Madding Crowd*. From now on Hardy is a professional novelist.

1874 September: Hardy and Emma Gifford marry in Paddington, London. They honeymoon in France.

1885 After various homes in London and Dorset, the Hardys move into newly-built Max Gate in Dorchester.

1886   *The Mayor of Casterbridge* is published.

1887   Spring: The Hardys tour Italy.

1891   *Tess of the D'Urbervilles* is published.

1892   Thomas Hardy's father dies.

1895   *Jude the Obscure* is published and received by critics and public with disgust at its obscenity. Emma Hardy, too, is deeply upset by it.

1896   Hardy decides not to write any more novels; *Jude the Obscure* was his last.

1898   *Wessex Poems*, Hardy's first collection of poems – dating back to the 1860s – is published.

1904   Thomas Hardy's mother dies.

1907   He meets Florence Dugdale, aged twenty-eight.

1908   He refuses knighthood.

1910   Florence Dugdale stays at Max Gate for a time and works as Hardy's secretary. Hardy is awarded the Order of Merit and the Freedom of Dorchester.

1912   27 November: Emma Hardy dies. December: Florence Dugdale comes to live at Max Gate.

1913   March: Hardy re-visits St Juliot, the Cornish village where he met Emma, and Plymouth, Emma's birthplace.

1914   February: Florence Dugdale and Thomas Hardy marry at Enfield, near London.

1915   Hardy's closest sister, Mary, dies.

1927   His last collection of poems, *Winter Words,* completed.

1928   11 January: Thomas Hardy dies. His ashes are buried in Westminster Abbey and his heart at Stinsford.